THIS FAR NORTH

T0164166

Also by Jason Tandon

THIS FAR NORTH

JASON TANDON

www.blacklawrence.com

Executive Editor: Diane Goettel
Book Design: Amy Freels
Cover Design: Zoe Norvell
Cover Art: "Snow Hut" by Scott Reither

Published 2023 by Black Lawrence Press.
Printed in the United States.

for my family

It's all right if we keep forgetting the way home.
It's all right if we don't remember when we were born.
It's all right if we write the same poem over and over.

—Robert Bly, "What Did We See Today?"

Contents

II

III

I

People Talking

This morning I awoke
to the sound of people talking.
I got dressed,
buttoned my shirt
to the top. People
still talking.

Poem

The children bend
cattail stems,
squeeze the sponges
of flower and fruit.

They kneel
to smear their cheeks
with scoops of sulfurous mud.

Man Paddling Canoe with Dog

The sky so white
there is no sky.
The water,
a tarnished plate of silver.

The dog sits dutifully.
No, sits like a king
who says nothing,
who looks around
unmoved,

his golden robe
shedding.

After Time Away

Along the slate path
the ants have dug their tunnels,

displaced the dirt
into little mounds,
fresh graves.

Here I come,
black jug
with tube and trigger
filled with chemical rain.

For Keats

In the hag-like hair
of a gangrenous birch
that leans
as if gazing
            into the lake

a crow, a cloud
entangled.

My Hand in the Lamplight

My hand
in the lamplight
has good color,
is rosy in the joints.

My hand
in the lamplight
shakes.
I spread my fingers,
widen my palm.

My hand
in the lamplight
has good color
and shakes.

December 31st

Too cold
to drag your sled
across the frozen lake,
auger the hole

and chisel it wider.
Too cold
to sit in a shanty shack,
drink beer,
tell a joke

and drop your line
into
the lapping blackness.

Sunrise, Five Below

"What do you want to be
when you grow up?"
they asked.

The frozen tracks of snowshoes
heading into the spruce.

January Bramble

Like a remnant coil
of concertina wire

from which a sparrow easily leaps.

Ūrdhva Mukha Svānāsana

Looking up
out the basement window

I see the screen
has been clawed
by some small animal

that fell
into the well

in a blinding
winter storm.

I Came Here

after Du Fu

I came here to write a poem
and all I can do is look
at the beam of a solstice moon
lying across the lake.
I came here to write a poem.
All I can do
is listen

to the warped booms of water
under its own
frozen weight.

Driving Down to the Casino, I Think of You Grieving for Your Dead Father

From a speeding distance
the field was a sheet of hammered brass

though where I sit, having stepped
the muddy gully,

is greening.

Once More to the Lake

The gray squirrel who is with me
zig-zags the same patch of grass.
It snuffs the earth.
Scrapes up a nut.
Grips it.

Old Man Wets Himself at the Grocery Store

The look
on his face
we have seen

in paintings of angels
beholding

Today I Saw a Rainbow

Today I saw a rainbow,
the whole arc
for the first time, the entire spectrum of color
spanning the lake.

You could tell me about reflection and refraction,
droplets, dispersion, and sun—I paddled the western shore
looking for that goddamn pot.

Thinking about Laughter

Evenings I shrink
in a wingback chair
crinkling the daily paper.
"Don't blame me," my mother says.
My father coughs and clears his throat.

At the Office

Auroral
in the day's
last light

a cluster of dust
hovers above
a succulent plant

in a too-small pot
on the sill.

A Tank Away

*for Anthony Everett, Shayna Seymour, and
Ted Reinstein*

We sit
on the hotel balcony
in chairs not yet stowed
for the season.
The afternoon birds
depart the river's inlet,
the cormorant and blue heron.
Cushioned and reclined,

our kids count stars.

This Far North

Sprawled upon a granite slab
above the no-name falls
my friend tells about his dream last night.

He knows he felt
failure and menace,
anger and injustice—
he can't remember
the people or the place.

He breaks a bar of chocolate
from his backpack.
We lay our socks in the sun.

Blue Skies, Calm Water

All day long
a beeping steamroller
in reverse.

What Is This Feeling I Get at the End of Every August?

It's those weeds I've never seen
standing tall.
They grow out of dust and stone.

It's when I stand
at the edge of the night trees
listening
to the insects scream.

Outdoor Shower

I haven't read the news
in a month. Haven't
touched the TV.
The water runs cold. The hot
never works.

Please Understand

When I woke
to my daughter
slapping my ear and sing-
shouting about the dolphin
she rode in her dream,
my son
upside down in the armchair
asking what the word
"vehemence" means,
and you
on the pillow
pale-faced, open-mouthed, dry-lipped and snoring—
I thought
if I must die
let it be now.

II

Poem

When I stop moving this pencil across the paper—

mice
scratching in the attic.

Morning Song

Above Chocorua's
craggy face
there is a thumb-sized
patch of blue,
the lake and low hills socked in by fog.

When I was a boy
that was all the start I needed
to rip this life
to shreds.

Coyote

It comes into the yard again,
trips the motion light.
Comes from the wood
behind the neighbor's
rickety barn
and skulks
to the edge
of our busy road.
Skulks and shrinks back
from where cars do not care
about kids crossing
and motorcycles drag after midnight.
Where sirens
scream at all hours
for there is always a fire,
a crime,
a shattered hip,
a toddler
choking on a grape
the mother
neglected to slice.

Not Writing

after Jane Kenyon

The hired men came in waders,
gaffed each plank
of our lone
delinquent dock
with a garden rake.

The wind blew.
The water churned.
The men
slipped and staggered.

Thanksgiving

Patting the skin
of this naked bird

reminds me of bathing our kids
in a plastic tub
that fit the kitchen sink.

What I Knew

after Robert Hayden

Walking Long Sands Road
we saw a red fox,
my son and I,
trot across our path
and leap
a frozen stream,

its coat
perfectly camouflaged
by what leaves still clung
to those late
November trees.

It Was Yesterday

It was yesterday I saw
the first snow fall
this new year,

large flakes
few
and far between,

not enough
to coat the roads
or whiten the grass—

winter,
a newborn child

whose cries
cause us no pain.

Writing

Those three screw heads
on the furnace filter panel
are loose and stripped.
Mornings I come down
to the back storage room
where I have a desk
and a green banker's lamp,
boxes of Mirado pencils
and yellow legal pads.
By now, when the furnace fires up,
I've grown used to those
three screw heads
and their high-pitched glee.

I Finally Tried It

in memory of Mary Oliver

On a hot spring day
when midges spawn and spasm
above the raked plots of dormant grass,
I filled the feeder
with an Eastern songbird blend—
black oil sunflower, cracked corn and millet—
removed my shoes, my socks,
lay down,
wiggled my toes,
and waited.

Spring Walk

Atop the fence's
rain-soaked gate

the inchworm's green arch

After a Week of News

My son turns nine
and there's bowling with bumpers,

dumplings and moo shu
at Mandarin Cuisine,

a homemade cake
with buttercream frosting

so rich, so sweet
we push back our plates

as if heaped with Brussels sprouts and broccoli.

Sunday

Seeing my neighbor
go out to the barn

and roll his mower
down the ramp

makes me pull on my pair
of canvas pants,

the ones with permanent stains.

Middle Life

It's been raining now
for three straight days.
Standing at the sink,
staring at the dark green grass,
the rotten fence, the absolute gray
of what sky we can see
between the houses and trees,
my wife asks,
"Tea?"

Birds Again

in memory of my student, 2000–2019

After last spring's
surprise grackle attack
and the autumn squirrels'
burgling
          acrobatics

I almost didn't fill
the feeders this year.

They came back,
the heavy-set doves
content to peck
what falls in the dirt,
the bullying blue jays,
the cardinal—always so startling
to see that red,
that beak blot
of orange.

Ten Thousand Apologies

When they fell,
the cherry blossoms,

and the wind and the rain
glued them
to the siding and stoop,
the car, driveway, and roof,

What a mess, I thought.

Beacon/Flower

My daughter picks
a dandelion, calls it
"a bouquet"
and asks for a vase.
I explain

the yellow flower
is a beacon
that shows it must be
pronged by the root,
always by the root

before it blooms into seed
and is blown
by the slightest breeze.

Back Fence

Too many posts now
rotted beneath the ground

from the bugs and rain and lingering
drifts of snow,

props of mitered boards
all askew.

In a mild March wind
the panels pitch

and lean
as I open the shed

to the funk of mice,
a forgotten

bag of grass.

April Snow

Between the soft
coo-coos
of the mourning dove

I hear the tick-
tick-tick against the pane.

Walden

Struck by the iron poker

the woodstove
a temple bell

Shakespeare

My inner critic says
there's nothing noble
about cutting the grass,
painting the fence,
installing a storm door
or shoveling snow—

though I might get a laugh
from the people up front,
the ones
penned in like cows,

when I end this poem
to plunge the toilet
upstairs.

For My Life

At the pond's sandy bar,
I strip
to my skin,
high-knee into the wintry water,
thrash.

III

What Happened Here?

for Charles Simic

Half a mouse
lying in the driveway,
the head and belly
hollowed out, a small pool
of black blood

where my daughter likes to draw
with her box of rainbow chalk
a unicorn
under the Tree of Magical Dreams.

Rabbits

They sit
in the front yard
nibbling broadleaf and clover,
and when I clap
or shout from an open window—

barely a sidelong glance
from a single, beady eye.

Just Once

Did I see
a praying mantis
on one of the deck chairs we bought
from a box store
when we moved in.

Now, years later, I am thinking
of that insect—I can't
picture it.

The deck chairs leak
rust from their frames
after rain.

The Dead of Summer

The backyard badminton net
sagging into a smile,

the brightly colored kayaks
overturned,

one inflated inner tube
lodged in the rocks,

the empty mooring
at the neighbor's next door

who, we were told,
got too sick
to travel.

Loons

Why is it such a pleasure
when they dive

to scan the surface for where
they might
         reappear

and be wrong
every time?

On the Farm

for my kids

The horses came into the barn
in the heat. They ate
candy canes and carrots
from our hands. If we didn't
hold them flat, the owner told us,
Midge would eat a finger.
We laughed. The owner did not.

Retirement, Day One

A bank of cloud
a quarter-mile long

like an endless herd of sheep
stopping traffic
on a single country lane.

Retirement, Day Two

Now that I can stare
at the glittering path of sunlight
cast upon the lake,

it looks like the bursting
of a hundred antique flash bulbs

as if some long-legged
somebody
is taking her time
entering the ball.

Why Now Do I Wish to Live on a Cliff by the Sea?

When I was a boy
I was afraid of sharks,
was stung by a jellyfish.
Once, standing in the Sound,
what I thought
was a floor of broken shells

were crabs
without claws
scattering laterally.

The Hike

after a line by Galway Kinnell, and
for my son

We squat
on a bench
missing its middle slat,
tear jerky with our teeth.
What we don't know

is the fountain a mile off,
the pistol spigot
that will ice
our spines at the root.
What we don't know

is the sight of the first chalet
sloped above town,
shutters flung wide to the open air,

and the boxes beneath them
frothing with flowers
in the sop
of summer's heat.

For My Mother and Father

The concrete Buddha
propped on a pedestal of paving stones

has moved from many houses
into many new yards

and now sits,
robe blackened by weather and time,

with its back
to the lake, blue hills

and mountains beyond.

How Do I Love Thee?

Old woman
entering the sea,
you float alone
in the frigid water,
your towel
balled in the sand. You brought
nothing else,

pale speck
in a gunmetal swell.

Lines on My Forty-Fourth Birthday

The sun up
for an hour or so, I hear
thumping upstairs,
my son's strong stream
of urine in the bowl.
I see the first boat
anchor in the shallows,

some brave soul
who called in sick,
took one day
to fish.

Daylight Savings

Resting my hands
on the rake
I watch the crimped
brown bags lined along the road,

a faceless crowd in coats
waiting on a bus
or bread.

I Had Wanted to Write

I had wanted to write
about the light in late November,
the afternoon light
that slaps the sides of houses,
stays low and gold.

This year, looking closer,
I see beneath the leaf
a red tincture.
My human heart
beats its blood
into the light of late November.

There We Were

*for Ryan, Justin, Andrew, William,
and Craig*

Hunched against the railing,
gazing at the river and the city skyline,

one of us imagined jumping
onto a truck below

and riding the roof
back home.

One of us brought up
the towers,

wondered what the air
must have smelled like,

the screaming in the sky.
One of us

talked about ramps and remodeling
for a son who woke

with a headache
and had not walked

or talked
since.

One of us scuffed his sole
against the curb,

told about the bridge,
the men with the bends

who dug to the bedrock.
One of us said

there was ice cream nearby.
Our backs hurt.
It was breakfast time.

Poem

Each time
the chipmunk scurries
from under the deck to a hole in the yard
it carries a nut
the size of its head
between its paws.

Back and forth it bounds
preparing
for winter.

The Fourth

July 2020

A full moon rose
over the lake, the kids
tangled in sleep on the floor.

Arms, knees, torsos
twisted in the moonlight

like statues
fallen from their plinths.

The Dead of Summer

after Rainer Brambach

The dragonfly
that has landed
on the pillow of this pink vinyl raft
with its lightning blue body,
planetary eyes,
four wings spread ready for flight,

lifts into the breeze
backwards, diagonally.

This must be
what gave da Vinci
his helicopter concept.

Surely, he was standing
neck-deep in water.

Out Here, at the Edge of the Land

At First Light

I walk the splintered boardwalk
smoothed by wind and sand, salt and morning mist

and climb the crest
of a whale-backed dune. I sit

and scratch bites
on my unwashed body,

bleed every itch.

Bay Side

Today
I will not realize
that my friend
drowned at twenty-one
would have turned
forty-six,

even when I find
that silver fish
pumping its gills on the sandbar,
its black eyes
surprised by the tide.

Dog Days

I look into the mirror's
small square
and see my face
stubbled white,
hair thick with sweat,
nose greased
and blistered at the tip,
my chapped lips
grinning ear to ear.

It Was the Mourning Doves

It was the mourning doves
that woke me
hidden in the pitch pines
and the rattling click
of a black crow. When I woke

it was the honey bee I saw
entering the clover

and the monarch butterfly
fluttering above me
as I swam far
from shore.

Robins, 6 A.M.

They hop
two-footed
in the dewy grass, one
after the other. He
pulls a worm from the earth.
She gobbles it whole.
Neither wonders
what is next.

Visiting My Parents in the New Year, We Take the Children Sledding

Day's end
we lie in a blue-black tinge.
Our breathing
slows
to a silence.

Sometimes
your child drops the sled
and you must trudge back down
to retrieve it.

Driving to the Package Store So I Don't Have to Go One Evening without a Beer, I See the Full Moon Massive and White and Shaded with Craters and Realize for the First Time in a Long Time, I Live on a Planet in Space

Notes

"Ūrdhva Mukha Svānāsana" is Sanskrit for "Upward-Facing Dog," a yoga posture in the Sun Salutation sequence.

"A Tank Away" is a program on WCVB-TV's *Chronicle* that highlights a travel destination within 175 miles of Boston, Massachusetts. The dedication names the regular hosts.

The line referred to in "The Hike" is from Galway Kinnell's poem "La Bagarède" from his book *Body Rags*: "The black / water I gulp from the spring / hits my brain at the root."

Acknowledgments

I am grateful to the editors and staffs of the following publications, in which some of these poems first appeared:

The Aurorean: "Once More to the Lake"

Beloit Poetry Journal: "Visiting My Parents in the New Year, We Take the Children Sledding"

Cave Wall: "After Time Away," "Driving Down to the Casino, I Think of You Grieving for Your Dead Father"

Columbia Poetry Review: "People Talking"

Faultline: "December 31st," "Why Now Do I Wish to Live on a Cliff by the Sea?"

Good River Review: "Shakespeare"

Kestrel: "Daylight Savings," "How Do I Love Thee?"

The Laurel Review: "At the Office," "Driving to the Package Store So I Don't Have to Go One Evening without a Beer, I See the Full Moon Massive and White and Shaded with Craters and Realize for the First Time in a Long Time, I Live on a Planet in Space," "My Hand in the Lamplight," "Not Writing," "Thinking about Laughter"

The Louisville Review: "I Finally Tried It," "Loons"

The Midwest Quarterly: "For Keats," "Retirement, Day One," "Retirement, Day Two," "Walden," "What I Knew"

Modern Haiku: "Spring Walk" (originally published without title)

Jason Tandon is the author of five books of poetry, including *This Far North*, *The Actual World*, *Quality of Life*, and *Give Over the Heckler and Everyone Gets Hurt*, winner of the St. Lawrence Book Award from Black Lawrence Press. His poems have appeared in *Ploughshares*, *Prairie Schooner*, *The Southern Review*, *Alaska Quarterly Review*, and *Beloit Poetry Journal*, among others. He teaches in the Arts & Sciences Writing Program at Boston University.

Nixes Mate Review: "What Happened Here?"

North American Review: "After a Week of News," "Coyote"

Ploughshares: "Man Paddling Canoe with Dog"

Poet Lore: "Sunrise, Five Below," "The Dead of Summer (The dragonfly)," "This Far North"

Poetry East: "For My Mother and Father," "Poem (When I stop moving)," "Please Understand," "Ūrdhva Mukha Svānāsana"

Prairie Schooner: "Out Here, at the Edge of the Land"

RHINO: "Writing"

Ruminate: "I Had Wanted to Write"

Salamander: "Birds Again"

Salt Hill: "Morning Song," "Poem (The children bend)," "What Is This Feeling I Get at the End of Every August?"

Southern Poetry Review: "January Bramble," "Middle Life," "Ten Thousand Apologies"

The Southern Review: "The Hike," "There We Were"

Tar River Poetry: "Back Fence," "The Dead of Summer (The backyard badminton net)"

Water~Stone Review: "I Came Here"

Wildness (U.K.): "A Tank Away," "It Was Yesterday"

"January Bramble" was also reprinted in the *Southern Poetry Review*, vol. 55, no. 2, a special issue on the short poem.